GUIDE TO
DIVING CATALINA ISLAND

By

Bruce Wicklund

Published by

BLACK DOLPHIN DIVING

Catalina Island, California

1995

First Edition

Library of Congress Catalog Card Number 95-94107
International Standard Book Number 0-9646281-3-9

Printed in the United States of America by
Southern California Graphics, Culver City, California

From Sea Fever

And a gray mist on the sea's face, and a
*   gray dawn breaking.*
I must go down to the sea again, for the call of the
*   running tide*
Is a wild call and a clear call that may not be denied;

By John Masefield

Special thanks to: Cindy Spring
                     Jim Walker
                     Dave Carpenter
                     Jim Morrow
                     Carol and Rainer Lorch
                     The Cherry Cove Out to Lunch Bunch

Cover, back cover and center flap photos by David Erwitt
(Phud Lee Photos)

Top and bottom flap photos by Dave Lieberman

TABLE OF CONTENTS

PREFACE

This book attempts to answer some of the questions about Catalina Island diving. Simple common names and places familiar to Islanders are used. The drawings of Catalina and various dive locations are for general reference and are not intended for use in navigation. Although not to scale, the dive site drawings show the general reef layout and will provide a good start toward planning a dive. Following a dive, log in any specific observations for future reference.

When hunting game, practice conservation and observe all Fish and Game rules and regulations. Pay attention to special tools, measuring devices, size and bag limits. Be sure to read the F & G section on Invertebrates before taking lobster, abalone and scallops. Be aware of special closed areas and marine preserves.

Many divers visit Catalina every year, so common sense and safety are important. Spearfishing, caves, wrecks and deep diving sites, mentioned in the "Where to Dive" section may require special skills and training before diving. Divers are responsible for using safe diving procedures within personal limitations. Hopefully the information and opinions provided will enhance the enjoyment and safety of diving at Catalina Island.

I. CATALINA INFORMATION

General information on geography, history,
marine life and wrecks of Catalina Island.

INTRODUCTION TO CATALINA

Santa Catalina Island was formed long ago by colliding earth plates and volcanic activity. Originally located off the coast of Mexico, Catalina is slowly moving up the California coast. The island is 22 miles long and 7 miles across at its widest point. The climate is moderate and similar to mainland beach communities with a temperature range of 46 to 81 degrees. Prevailing west winds may change to northeast (Santa Ana) from October to early Spring. The rainy season extends from November to April and averages about 12 inches per year. Catalina is the second largest of the eight Channel Islands.

About 7,000 years ago, Indian hunter/gatherers naturally migrated to the island. The largest communities were located at Emerald Bay, Two Harbors, Little Harbor and Avalon. Later, the Pimu Indians developed a thriving soapstone industry at Empire Landing, whose artifacts remain. Cabrillo discovered the island for Spain in 1542 and named it San Salvador. Sixty years later, Vizcaino rediscovered the island and named it Santa Catalina after St. Catherine. In the late 1700's, Aleut Indians were brought in to hunt the sea otters. Aleut attacks and disease decimated the local Indian population. In 1846, the last Mexican Governor of California was rumored to have granted the title to Catalina in trade for a fresh horse and a silver saddle during his final retreat to Mexico. When the Mexican American War ended in 1848, California and the Channel Islands became part of American territory.

During the Civil War, the Fourth Infantry of California Volunteers fortified the Isthmus at Two Harbors. Several large production movies were filmed at Catalina including "The Black Pirate" and "Old Ironsides." The buffalo that roam Catalina today are descendants of the original fourteen brought over for the 1925 Zane Grey movie "The Vanishing American." During World War II, the military maintained guns and bunkers at Ben Weston Point and training barracks at Camp Cactus.

Tales of treasure, sunken galleons, piracy, smugglers and lost gold abound. Catalina has been ranched, farmed, mined, bought, sold and resold. Fourteen owners have claimed title to the island. Finally in 1919, William Wrigley Jr. joined a syndicate to purchase Catalina Island, sight unseen. Upon visiting the island and falling in love with it, he then bought the remaining interest. William Wrigley Jr. developed the island as an affordable vacation destination. His vision and plan for the future of Catalina Island was that it remain protected for all generations. Therefore, it was fitting when in 1975, William Wrigley Jr.'s descendants donated 86 percent of the island to the Santa Catalina Island Conservancy, a non-profit foundation. Today the Conservancy is involved in restoring Catalina Island to its natural state.

Just a short distance from the southern California mainland (19 miles) makes Catalina Island a convenient resort. Numerous activities are available including camping, hiking, bicycling, horseback riding, golf, tennis, fishing, kayaking and parasailing. For divers, 54 miles of rugged coastline provide sheer drops, reefs, pinnacles, caves, lush kelp beds and marine life. Waters are clear and visibility may exceed 80 feet, although summer plankton blooms may decrease visibility. Water temperature ranges from 64 to 73 degrees in summer and 54 to 59 degrees in winter. Catalina Island offers a variety of year-round diving. Enjoy it and help protect its resources.

KELP DIVING

Kelp comes in many varieties, but kelp diving refers to giant kelp. Secured to rocks by a holdfast and suspended by gas-filled bladders at the base of the fronds, kelp resembles an enchanted forest. Diving the kelp beds is easy and enjoyable when a few skills are mastered. Practice snorkeling around the kelp bed and discover the open channels that wind through the canopy. Use slow deliberate movements and be aware of the surroundings. Touch, smell and taste it (yum!). Pull and stretch it like a rubber band. Roll and wrap in it like a sea otter, then relax and feel it loosen. Swim over the canopy by using a small flutter kick while pushing the kelp under the body with the arms (kelp crawl).

Before diving, take compass bearings for underwater navigation. Observe the kelp signs to determine reef size, visibility and current. Streamline loose gear. Place knife inside leg, secure octopus regulator, trim excess straps, turn fin straps in and tuck the console inside the buoyancy compensator. Be aware of hanging objects such as cameras and spearguns.

Diving under kelp is easier due to greater spacing. "Dive with the flow and watch where you go" to avoid entanglements. Getting caught is normal. Stay calm; it's no problem. Whenever movement is restricted by a tugging feeling, just relax, reach back and untangle it. Still hung up? Give a quick jerk to snap the kelp or get a buddy to help. If all else fails, slowly use a knife to cut the kelp or remove the entangled equipment. Keep at least 500 PSI air in reserve to navigate out of the kelp bed. To surface inside the bed, locate a gap in the canopy and use exhaust bubbles to expand the opening or use arms to part the kelp. To descend, exhaust the BC and drop down feet first. On the surface it's often easier to swim around the kelp or use the kelp crawl to go over. Catalina's best diving is in and around the kelp, so get used to it and have some fun.

MARINE PLANTS & ALGAE

Most of the plants encountered by divers are algae. Algae is divided into groups by color. Green algae (G) is green colored, small to medium in size and mostly found in intertidal water. Red algae (R) is reddish colored and may display purple, yellow, green or brown shades. Brown algae (B) is brown colored, largest of all algae and abundant off the California coast. Also a few flowering plants (P), eel and surf grasses, inhabit the shallow water.

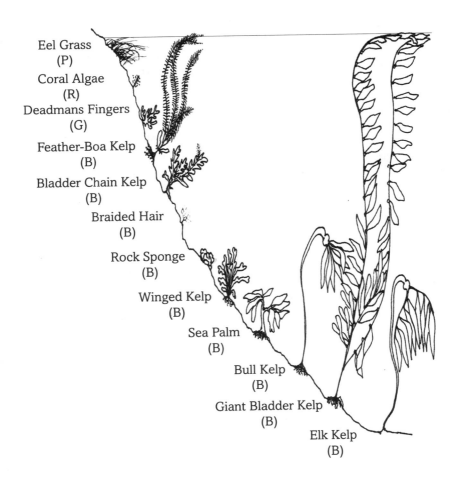

Eel Grass (P)
Coral Algae (R)
Deadmans Fingers (G)
Feather-Boa Kelp (B)
Bladder Chain Kelp (B)
Braided Hair (B)
Rock Sponge (B)
Winged Kelp (B)
Sea Palm (B)
Bull Kelp (B)
Giant Bladder Kelp (B)
Elk Kelp (B)

FISH

BLUEBANDED GOBY
Bright orange/red body with 3 to 6 bright blue (zebra) stripes. Length to 2 1/2".

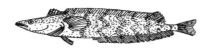

KELPFISH
Long snout and body. Color varies to match background (similar to blade of kelp). Length to 24".

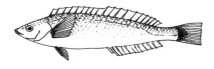

SENORITA
Cigar-shaped with yellow/orange color. Black spot at tail. Length to 12".

BARRACUDA
Long and thin with many sharp teeth. Silvery color with yellow tail. Length to 48".

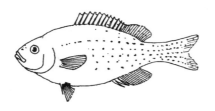

BLACKSMITH
Dark blue color with black spots at back and tail. Small mouth. Length to 12".

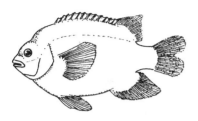

GARIBALDI
Bright orange color. Small juveniles have bright blue spots. Length to 14".

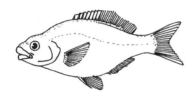

RUBBERLIP PERCH
Brassy brown color. Large thick lips. Length to 18".

TREEFISH
Rockfish. Yellow color with dark vertical bars and pink lips. Length to 16".

HALFMOON
Blue color with small mouth. Sleek looking with half moon shaped tail. Length to 18".

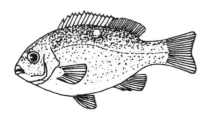

OPALEYE
Green/blue color with 2 white spots on back. Length to 20".

SHARKS & RAYS

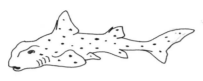

HORN SHARK
Lives on bottom. Brown with dark spots. Rounded horns on head. Spine in front of each dorsal fin. Female lays olive green corkscrew egg cases in crevasses. Length to 48".

SWELL SHARK
Lives on the bottom, in caves and crevasses. Mottled brown color with plump belly. Can inflate its stomach to swell in size when disturbed. Female lays amber colored egg cases. Length to 40".

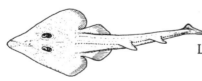

GUITARFISH
Lives on sand bottoms in shallow water. Long tail and shape similar to guitar. Length to 60".

THORNBACK
Lives on sand and mud bottoms. Three rows of spines on back and tail. Two dorsal fins on tail. Length to 30".

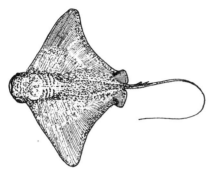

BAT RAY
Lives on sand and mud
bottoms. Large blunt head
with pointed tail. Length to
60" (body width is about the
same as length).

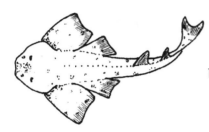

ANGEL SHARK
Lives on sand and mud
bottoms. Large head with
broad wings and brown spots.
Length to 60".

LEOPARD SHARK
Lives on sand and mud
bottoms. Large spots and bars
on back. Length to 80".

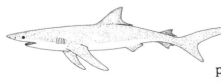

BLUE SHARK
Lives in open ocean. Long
pointed nose. Blue back with
gray/white belly. Long swept
back tail. Length to 156".

SHELLS

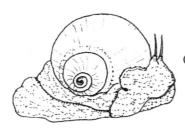

MOON SNAIL
Lives on sand or mud. Thick tan shell shaped like a ball. Giant-sized foot. Lays eggs in a sand encrusted collar. Diameter to 6".

BROWN TURBAN
Found on kelp and brown algae. Smooth reddish-brown shell with pearl white inside. Foot is black with orange rim. Height to 2".

WAVY TURBAN
Lives on rock and sand bottoms. Shell has wavy spiral ridge, ornate markings and covered by a brown skin and marine growth. Inside shell is pearl white. Height to 5".

LEAFY HORNMOUTH
Brown and white colored, often banded. Three winged murex. Length to 4".

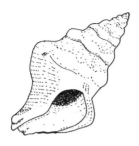

WELK
Lives on rocks and sand.
Thick white to tan colored
shell. Very common at
Catalina. Length to 8".

CHESTNUT COWRIE
Smooth glossy shell with white
sides and brown patch on top.
Reddish brown mantle may
cover shell. Length to 3".

MUSSEL
Lives in shallow water attached
to rocks and pilings etc... Purple
shell covered with a black skin.
Length to 10".

KEYHOLE LIMPET
Lives on rocky reefs. Shield
shaped shell with oval hole.
Body is brown mottled to black
and often covers shell. Foot is
similar to abalone. Length to 7".

MARINE LIFE

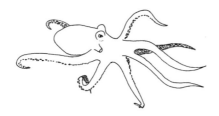

OCTOPUS
Found hiding in rocks. Can
change color and texture.
Length to 30".

SEA CUCUMBER
Reddish-brown in color with
tube feet. Length to 16".

BRITTLE STAR
Found under rocks. Wide
range of types and sizes.
Diameter to 6".

SEA STAR
Lives on rocky reefs.
Randomly spaced, white
tipped spines with blue ring at
base. Length to 22".

GRAY MOON SPONGE
Smooth gray sponge with
moon-like craters on outer
ridge. Attached to rocks.

TUBE ANEMONE
Dark bumpy tube. Long whip-like tentacles in a wide range of colors. Size to 12" high and 2" diameter.

SEA ANEMONE
Deep to pale green color. Lives in mid to low tidal areas attached to rocks and crevasses. Diameter to 6".

SEA HARE

Lives in rocky and sandy areas. Mottled brown to dark purple in color. 2 flaps on back and 2 tentacle-like appendages on head (Similar to rabbit). Length to 18".

SPANISH SHAWL
Nudibranch with bright purple body and bright orange, hairlike appendages on back. Length to 2".

SPIDER CRAB
Oval shaped body with long legs. Gray to tan color. Often covered with marine growth. Length to 70".

HAZARDOUS MARINE LIFE

SEA URCHIN
Long sharp spines which may
puncture and break off.

BARNACLE
Secured to rocks and pilings,
Sharp cutting edges.

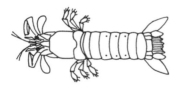

MANTIS SHRIMP
Dangerous razor sharp
appendages. Live in holes on
sandy bottom. Purplish tail
similar to that of lobster.

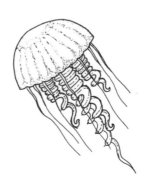

JELLYFISH
Live at the surface and mid
water. Stinging tentacles.
Carefully clean the affected
area. Use of vinegar may help.

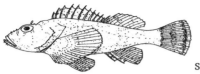

SCORPIONFISH
(SCULPIN)
Well camoflaged on the bottom. Sharp poisonous spines. If punctured, soak with hot water to relieve pain.

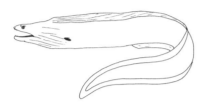

MORAY EEL
Live in holes. Have sharp teeth, a good sense of smell and poor eyesight. Avoid sticking hands in holes and carrying game.

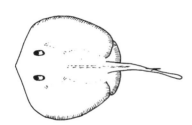

STINGRAY
Live on sand or mud bottoms. Have a sharp barb at the end of the tail. Avoid stepping on them when entering water by shuffling feet. Soak with hot water to relieve pain.

TORPEDO RAY
Large round head and body. Mottled grayish-brown color. Lives on mud or sand bottom or may be free swimming. Can be aggressive and deliver up to 80 volts electric charge. Avoid contact.

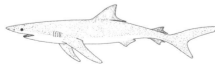

SHARK
Have sharp teeth. Be aware when carrying bloody fish. Avoid contact.

WRECKS

Indians crossed the channel in plank canoes. Spanish ships traded along the route from Manila to Mexico. Otter hunters and smugglers plied the waters for profit. Yachts traveled to the island resort for relaxation. Many were lost or stranded in storms. Some were accidentally destroyed by fire or torched for a movie scene. Most of the wrecks listed have deteriorated, scattered or disappeared. Researching Catalina shipwreck history is often confusing and misleading. The following information is composed from several sources.

SPANISH GALLEONS
From 1565 to 1815, the Manila galleons sailed California's waters. Several Spanish galleons and frigates have been reported or rumored to be lost around Catalina Island. Many efforts have been made to locate some of the wrecks, but have thus far been unsuccessful. Possibilities include the SAN SEBASTIAN: Galleon foundered west of Catalina in January, 1754 with gold, silver and oriental treasure; NUESTRA SENORA AYUDA: Galleon foundered west of Catalina in 1641 with treasure worth $500,000; SANTA CECILIA: Frigate foundered September, 1852, off Ship Rock with cargo valued at $100,000; SANTA MARTA: Stranded at Catalina with cargo valued at $100,000; SAN PEDRO: Manila galleon wrecked and sank in 14 fathoms at Arrow Point Reef? Gold and silver cargo worth over $2 million. Wreckage may have washed ashore in 1602 and in 1850 parts of the hull possibly discovered in 6 fathoms at Ship Rock.

1832   JOSEPHINE. Wrecked at Catalina.
1890   ALEUT. Tug
       Total loss ashore at Catalina on Nov. 12. One dead.
1891   FAWN. Sloop.
       Lost in a gale at Catalina on February 8. Two dead.
1908   PALMYRA. Clipper. Built 1876.
       Burned at Catalina. Remains of hull visible at low tide.
1920   NORTH STAR. Wrecked at Catalina on November 4.
1924   TAURUS. Four masted 551-ton schooner. Built 1902.
       Burned for a motion picture at Catalina on July 31.

1924 PROSPER. Three-masted 241-ton schooner. Built 1892.
Burned for a motion picture at Catalina on August 2.

1924 ALPINE. 95-ton. Built 1892. Burned at Avalon in October 29.

1926 CHARLES F. CROCKER. Four masted, 860-ton barkentine.
Built 1890. Foundered at Catalina.

1926 WILLIAM G. IRWIN. 348-ton barkentine. Built 1881.
Burned for a motion picture at Catalina on May 15.

1926 S. N. CASTLE . Three masted, 514-ton schooner. Built 1886.
Burned for a motion picture at Catalina on May 15.

1926 LLEWELLYN J. MORSE. 1392-ton ship. Built 1877.
Burned at Catalina on September 11. Filmed in the motion
picture "The Black Pirate" and portrayed
U.S.F. CONSTITUTION in "Old Ironsides."

1930 VALIANT. 163 feet long, 444-ton steel motoryacht.
Built 1926. One of the largest private yachts in the world at
the time. Exploded, burned and then sank off Descanso
Beach on December 17. Reported loss of $67,000 in jewels.
Wreck lies perpendicular to shore, listing to port with stern at
80 feet and bow at 110 feet deep. Famous for brass coins
with inscription "Yacht Valiant/Good for one drink." Dive
permit required from Avalon Harbormaster.

1931 WINDWARD. 63-ton yawl. Built 1907.
Burned at Catalina on July 25.

1931 LADY ALTA. 102-ton yawl. Built 1930.
Burned at Catalina in September.

1932 ADVANCE. Three-masted schooner.
Sank at Catalina on September 8.

1933 MARGARET C.: 58-ton schooner. Built 1880.
Burned at Catalina on May 3.

MORE WRECKS

1937 KITKA. U.S. Ship.
Lost two miles offshore, on Northwest side of Catalina.
1937 PRONTO. Wrecked off Catalina on March 1.
1930s NING PO. Over 100-foot long chinese junk. Built in 1753 with
ironwood and camphor. Carved to resemble a sea monster.
Originaly named KIN TAI FOONG, she was the fastest ship in
Chinese waters. Notorious and bloody history included piracy,
smuggling and slavery. 158 pirates were once beheaded on her
deck. Seized by Col. Peter "Chinese" Gordon in 1861 and
renamed after the city of Ning Po. Sailed from Shanghai and
arrived in San Pedro in February, 1913, sailing 7,000 miles
across the Pacific in 58 days. Used in motion pictures, viewed
by sight-seers and finally sank at Ballast Point, Catalina Harbor.
Remains of the keel and ribs are visible in the mud at low tide.

The NING PO at Ballast Point, Catalina Harbor.

1941 RUBY. Three-masted, 345-ton schooner.
Built 1902. Wrecked at Catalina.
1941 BROTHERS. 54-ton scow. Built 1890.
Foundered at Pebbly Beach on October 10.
1943 CHICAGO. 75-ton. Built 1926.
Foundered four miles south of Catalina on December 15.
1947 ROSSINO II.
Wrecked on northwest side of Catalina on August 22.
1949 VASHON. Sank at Catalina in August.
1950 ONWARD. 51-ton. Built 1919. Burned 5 miles southwest of
Catalina Harbor on February 22. (33-22-00 N, 117-45-30 W.)
1952 BLUE SKY. 99-ton. Built 1930.
Burned 2.5 miles off east end of Catalina on November 17.
1954 NORTH HEAD. 50-ton. Burned at Catalina on September 25.
1955 BENJIE BOY. 64-ton. Built 1950.
Burned 2 miles south of west end of Catalina on April 13.
1956 GENEVIEVE H. II. 112-ton. Built 1937.
Burned 15 miles southeast of east end of Catalina on Jan. 12.
1956 SANTA ROSA. 50-ton steel vessel. Built 1950.
Foundered 12 miles southwest of Catalina on November 23.
1960 WTCO No. 17. 330-ton barge. Built 1927.
Foundered on September 17.
1960 ZEPHYR. 104-ton. Built 1938.
Burned 5 miles southwest of west end of Catalina Oct. 28.
1966 OLD TIMER. 81-ton. Built 1928.
Stranded at Avalon on January 17.
1980 SUJAC. 70 Feet long ferocement schooner.
Sank during a storm at Avalon in November.
Located at base of southeast buoy in Avalon Underwater
Park. Lies on starboard side, bow down, 60 to 90 feet deep,
with two holes in the hull.
1990 DIOSA DEL MAR. 90 feet long, 60-ton wooden schooner.
Built 1898. Wrecked during the annual Catalina Firemans' Race
at Ship Rock in July. Bow section, masts and debris remain.
Main wreckage is 25 feet deep and scattered down slope.

CATALINA ISLAND DIVE LOCATIONS

FRONT SIDE:

28 Seal Rocks
29 Rock Quarry / Jewfish Point
30 Little Farnsworth
31 Ring Rock / Lover's Cove
32 Casino Point Underwater Park
34 Frog Rock
35 Torqua Springs
36 Moonstone Cove
37 White's Landing / Hen Rock
38 Long Point / Pirates Cove
39 Italian Gardens
40 Twin Rocks / Eel Land
41 Little Gibraltar
42 Seal Point / Paradise Cove
43 Rippers Cove / Empire Landing
44 Yellowtail Point / Rock Quarry
45 Sea Fan Grotto / Crane Point
46 Blue Cavern Point
47 Harbor Reef
48 Bird Rock
49 Ship Rock
50 4th of July Cove / Cherry Cove
51 Lion Head Point
52 Eagle Reef
53 Eel Cove

54 Little Geiger & Big Geiger Cove
55 Howland's Landing / Emerald Point
56 Indian Rock
57 Arrow Point
58 Black Point / Johnson's Rock
59 West End (Land's End)

BACK SIDE:

60 Eagle Rock
61 Cactus Bay
62 Gull Rock / Ironbound Cove
63 Ribbon Rock
64 Whale Rock
65 Kelp Point
66 Cape Cortez
67 Lobster Bay
68 Catalina Head
69 Catalina Harbor / Pin Rock
70 Pedestal Rock
71 Fred Rock
72 Little Harbor
73 Sentinel Rocks
74 Farnsworth Bank
75 China Point
76 Salta Verde Point
77 Church Rock

26

II. WHERE TO DIVE

Catalina dive sites showing the general reef area and other information. Circumnavigate the island begining on the frontside at the east end, around the west end, then travel the backside, finally returning to the east end. See the Catalina fold-out map and index of dive sites on the back page. Map and dive sites not to scale.

SEAL ROCKS

Seals and sealions. Some lobster.
Poor visibility.

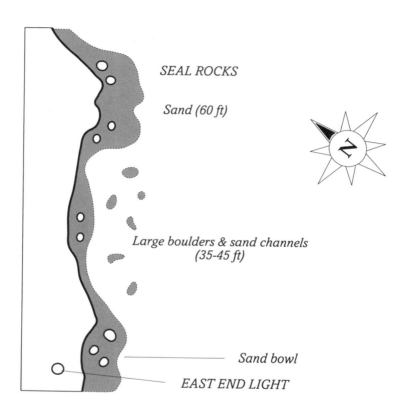

SEAL ROCKS

Sand (60 ft)

Large boulders & sand channels
(35-45 ft)

Sand bowl

EAST END LIGHT

Seal Rocks looking southwest.

ROCK QUARRY / JEWFISH POINT

*Jewfish Point named for a 500 pound black seabass
(now protected) caught there. Steep wall.
Dump and trees on hill. Lobster.
Beware of boat traffic and heavy currents.*

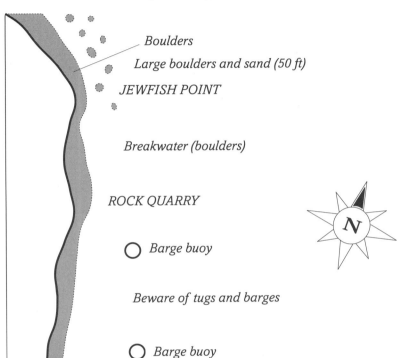

Boulders

Large boulders and sand (50 ft)

JEWFISH POINT

Breakwater (boulders)

ROCK QUARRY

Barge buoy

Beware of tugs and barges

Barge buoy

Rock quarry looking west.

LITTLE FARNSWORTH

*Rock pinnacle with peaks and cracks, about
75 yards offshore. Boat access only.
Depth finder required to locate. Beware of heavy boat traffic
and currents. Yellowtail, white seabass, calico, sheephead,
some scallops and lobster.*

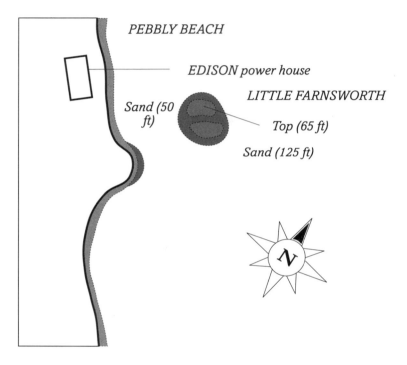

PEBBLY BEACH

EDISON power house

LITTLE FARNSWORTH

Sand (50 ft)

Top (65 ft)

Sand (125 ft)

From Little Farnsworth looking southwest to power house.

RING ROCK / LOVERS COVE

*Lovers Cove Marine Preserve has numerous
large friendly fish. Calico, sheephead
and schools of baitfish. Beach dive and snorkeling only (NO SCUBA).
Ring Rock marks end of boundary. Beware of boat traffic.
Boat debris. Spearfishing is discouraged (too close to preserve).*

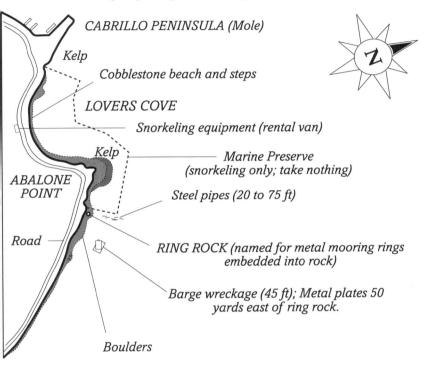

CABRILLO PENINSULA (Mole)

Kelp

Cobblestone beach and steps

LOVERS COVE

Snorkeling equipment (rental van)

Kelp

Marine Preserve
(snorkeling only; take nothing)

ABALONE
POINT

Steel pipes (20 to 75 ft)

Road

RING ROCK (named for metal mooring rings
embedded into rock)

Barge wreckage (45 ft); Metal plates 50
yards east of ring rock.

Boulders

Ring Rock and Abalone Point looking west.

CASINO POINT UNDERWATER PARK

Marine park: marked by buoys and rope (Take nothing). Numerous wrecks and marine life. Prevailing current is from the west. Beware of heavy boat traffic when outside of park. Dive permit required from Harbormaster prior to diving the Valiant or inside Avalon Harbor (no charge).

Author photographing the wreck of the Valiant.

Casino Point looking southwest.

DESCANSO BAY

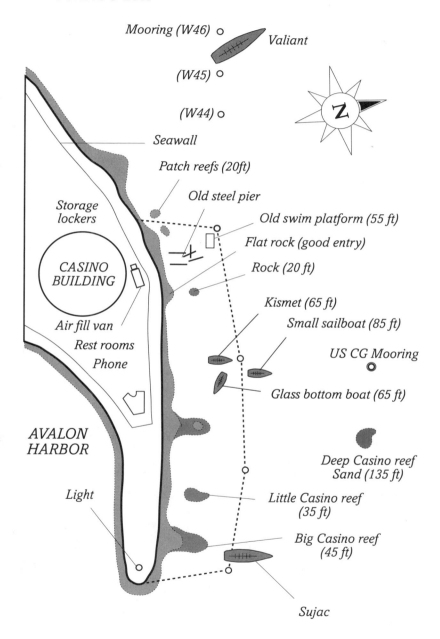

Mooring (W46)

Valiant

(W45)

(W44)

Seawall

Patch reefs (20ft)

Old steel pier

Storage lockers

Old swim platform (55 ft)

Flat rock (good entry)

CASINO BUILDING

Rock (20 ft)

Kismet (65 ft)

Small sailboat (85 ft)

Air fill van

Rest rooms

Phone

US CG Mooring

Glass bottom boat (65 ft)

AVALON HARBOR

Deep Casino reef
Sand (135 ft)

Light

Little Casino reef
(35 ft)

Big Casino reef
(45 ft)

Sujac

FROG ROCK

Scattered rocks and murky water.
Halibut, yellowtail and bat rays.

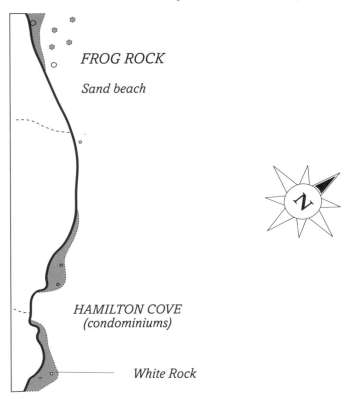

FROG ROCK

Sand beach

HAMILTON COVE
(condominiums)

White Rock

Frog Rock looking southwest.

TORQUA SPRINGS

Horseshoe-shaped reef about 150 yards long.
Moderate current. Murky at times.
Some lobster. Bat rays in sand.

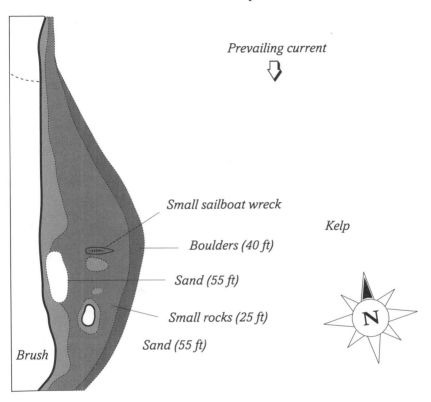

Prevailing current

Small sailboat wreck

Kelp

Boulders (40 ft)

Sand (55 ft)

Small rocks (25 ft)

Sand (55 ft)

Brush

N

Torqua Springs looking west.

MOONSTONE COVE

Moonstone Cove was named for the rounded rocks on the beach. Volcanic formations. Halibut and some lobster.

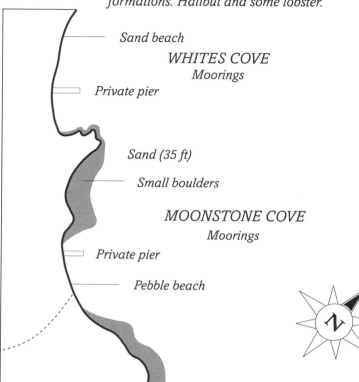

Sand beach

WHITES COVE
Moorings

Private pier

Sand (35 ft)

Small boulders

MOONSTONE COVE
Moorings

Private pier

Pebble beach

Moonstone Cove looking southwest.

WHITES LANDING & HEN ROCK

Hen Rock reef has large boulders and caves.
Currents and boat traffic.
Halibut, yellowtail and horn sharks.

Reef (large boulders)
Sand (70 ft)
Tunnel (20 ft)

Large boulders

HEN ROCK

N

Moorings

Tunnel through rock (5 ft)

WHITES LANDING
Moorings

Hen Rock looking southwest.

LONG POINT / PIRATES COVE

Shallow caves. Good anchorage in cove.
Heavy currents and boat traffic.
Halibut and some lobster.

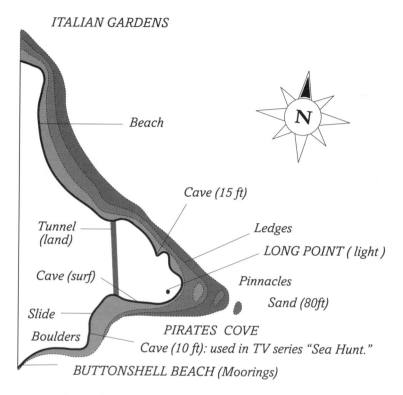

ITALIAN GARDENS

N

Beach

Cave (15 ft)

Tunnel
(land)

Ledges

LONG POINT (light)

Cave (surf)

Pinnacles

Sand (80ft)

Slide

Boulders

PIRATES COVE

Cave (10 ft): used in TV series "Sea Hunt."

BUTTONSHELL BEACH (Moorings)

Long Point looking northwest.

ITALIAN GARDENS

*Named for Italian fishermen drying nets
on the beaches. Scattered rock piles, caves,
cliffs and ledges. Halibut, calico,
sheephead, lobster and neon gobi.*

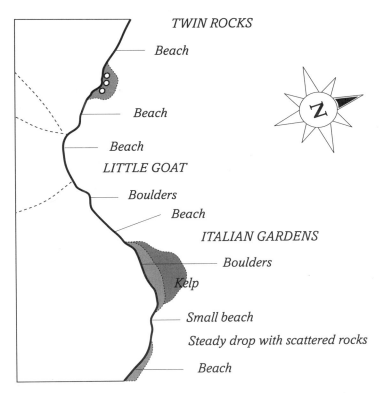

TWIN ROCKS

Beach

Beach

Beach

LITTLE GOAT

Boulders

Beach

ITALIAN GARDENS

Boulders

Kelp

Small beach

Steady drop with scattered rocks

Beach

Italian Gardens looking south.

39

TWIN ROCKS / EEL LAND

Rocky area from Twin Rocks to Eel Cove (look for eagles.) Goat Harbor has good anchorage and two Mongol huts (yurts) in canyon.

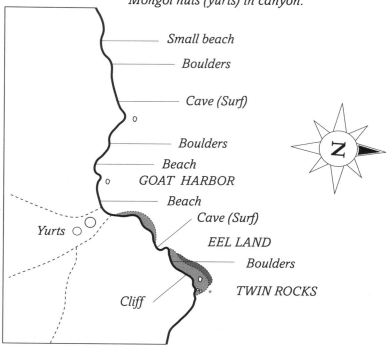

Small beach

Boulders

Cave (Surf)

Boulders

Beach

GOAT HARBOR

Beach

Cave (Surf)

EEL LAND

Yurts

Boulders

TWIN ROCKS

Cliff

N

Twin Rocks looking south.

LITTLE GIBRALTAR POINT

Sandy at Gibraltar with excellent anchorage off Cabrillo Beach. Caves at red lava rock points. Halibut, lobster and a few scallops.

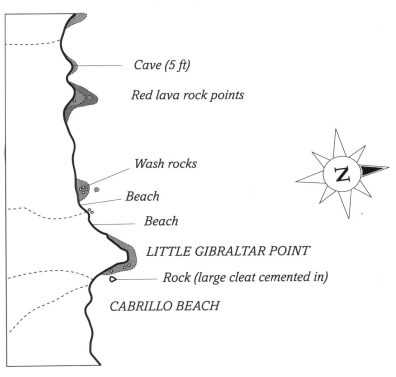

Cave (5 ft)

Red lava rock points

Wash rocks

Beach

Beach

LITTLE GIBRALTAR POINT

Rock (large cleat cemented in)

CABRILLO BEACH

Cabrillo Beach and Little Gibraltar Point looking south.

SEAL POINT / PARADISE COVE

Seals and sea lions on rocks.
Anchorage at Paradise Cove.

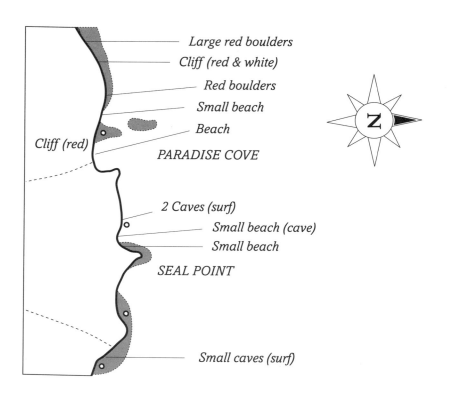

Large red boulders

Cliff (red & white)

Red boulders

Small beach

Beach

Cliff (red)

PARADISE COVE

2 Caves (surf)

Small beach (cave)

Small beach

SEAL POINT

Small caves (surf)

N

Seal Point looking south.

RIPPERS COVE / EMPIRE LANDING

Valley of the Ollas (canyon at Rippers)
site of Indian soapstone industry.
Good anchorage.
Halibut, calico and lobster.

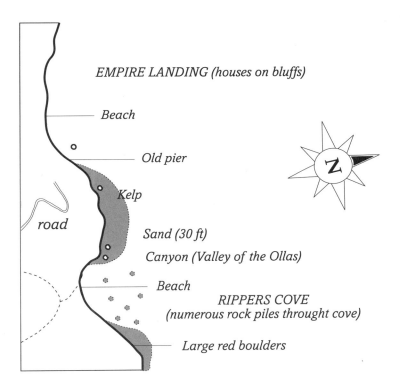

EMPIRE LANDING (houses on bluffs)

Beach

Old pier

Kelp

road

Sand (30 ft)

Canyon (Valley of the Ollas)

Beach

RIPPERS COVE
(numerous rock piles throught cove)

Large red boulders

Rippers Cove looking southwest.

YELLOWTAIL POINT / ROCK QUARRY

Yellowtail Point is shallow and rocky with some bull kelp. Anchorage is good at the point and deep off the quarry. Halibut, yellowtail and lobster.

ROCK QUARRY

Breakwater (steep drop off)

Gravel point

Shack

Beach

N

Road

Beach

Shallow rocky area

Small reef

Sand (30 ft)

Kelp

Sand (45 ft)

YELLOWTAIL POINT (Halfway reef)

Yellowtail Point looking southwest.

SEA FAN GROTTO / CRANE POINT

Marine preserve
Take nothing

BLUE CAVERN POINT

Cave & tunnel (surf to 15 ft)

PERDITION CAVES

Cliffs

Cave (surf)

Cliff
(red & white)

Steady drop off

SPOUTING CAVE

ROCKWELL PLATFORM
Top 150 feet,
Sandy base 175 feet.
Cables extend to shore (65 ft)

Cave (surf)

Boulders

SEA FAN GROTTO
Small rock formation at base
of white cliff. 4 caves (20 to 35 ft).
Cave with shaft to surface.
Gorgonians.

Boulders

Sand beach

Loading platform and cave (surf)

Breakwater

Kelp

Sand (65 ft)

Old crane base ○

CRANE POINT

Sea Fan Grotto looking southwest.

BLUE CAVERN POINT

*Lava formations, caves and currents.
Boat traffic. Difficult to anchor due to
depth and preserve.*

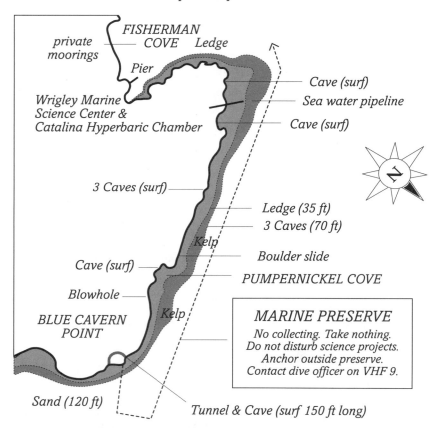

private moorings

FISHERMAN COVE   *Ledge*

Pier

*Wrigley Marine
Science Center &
Catalina Hyperbaric Chamber*

Cave (surf)

Sea water pipeline

Cave (surf)

3 Caves (surf)

Ledge (35 ft)

3 Caves (70 ft)

Kelp

Cave (surf)

Boulder slide

PUMPERNICKEL COVE

Blowhole

Kelp

*BLUE CAVERN
POINT*

MARINE PRESERVE

*No collecting. Take nothing.
Do not disturb science projects.
Anchor outside preserve.
Contact dive officer on VHF 9.*

Sand (120 ft)

Tunnel & Cave (surf 150 ft long)

Blue Cavern Point looking southwest.

46

HARBOR (ISTHMUS) REEF

Strong currents. Boat traffic. Some lobster.

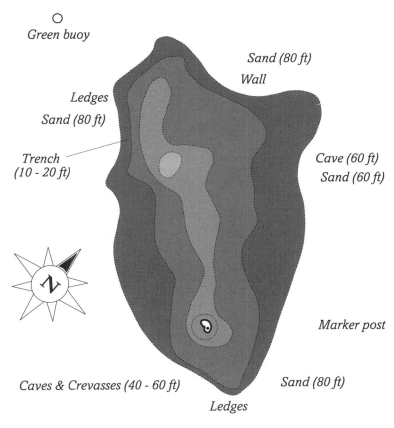

○
Green buoy

Sand (80 ft)

Wall

Ledges

Sand (80 ft)

Trench
(10 - 20 ft)

Cave (60 ft)

Sand (60 ft)

Marker post

Caves & Crevasses (40 - 60 ft)

Sand (80 ft)

Ledges

Harbor Reef looking northwest.

47

BIRD ROCK

*Privately owned. Once proposed
as site for gambling casino.
Currents and surge. Heavy boat traffic.
White seabass, yellowtail, halibut, calicos,
sheephead, lobster and some scallops.*

High spot (top 50 ft)

Sand (100 ft)

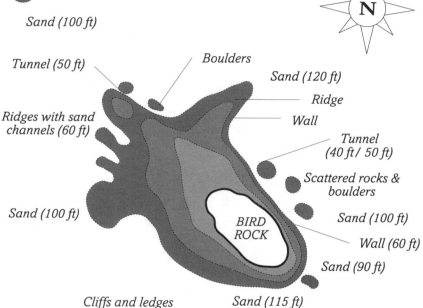

Tunnel (50 ft)   *Boulders*   *Sand (120 ft)*

Ridge

Ridges with sand channels (60 ft)   *Wall*

Tunnel (40 ft / 50 ft)

Scattered rocks & boulders

Sand (100 ft)   *Sand (100 ft)*

BIRD ROCK

Wall (60 ft)

Sand (90 ft)

Cliffs and ledges   *Sand (115 ft)*

N

Bird Rock looking northeast.

SHIP ROCK

Named for appearance similar to white sail.
Currents and surge. Heavy boat traffic.
White seabass, yellowtail, calico, sheephead,
lobster and scallops, sealions, seals, horn sharks and angel sharks.

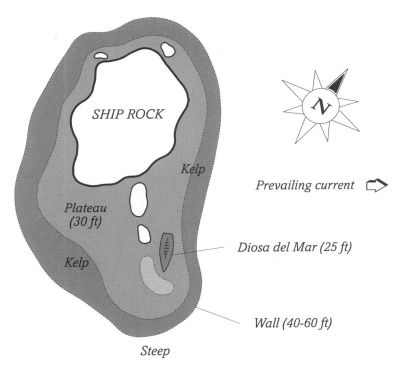

Ship Rock looking north.

FOURTH OF JULY & CHERRY COVE

Some lobster. Heavy boat traffic.

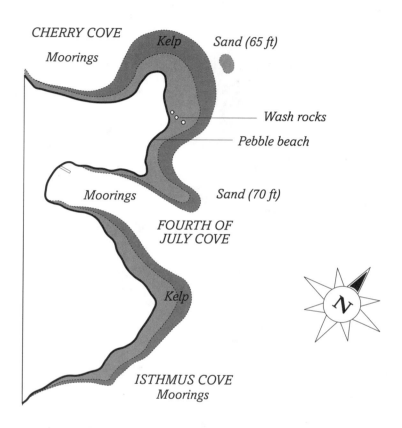

CHERRY COVE

Kelp

Sand (65 ft)

Moorings

Wash rocks

Pebble beach

Moorings

Sand (70 ft)

FOURTH OF
JULY COVE

Kelp

N

ISTHMUS COVE
Moorings

Fourth of July and Cherry Coves looking southwest.

LION HEAD POINT

Special closed area. Take no invertebrates.
Beware of boat traffic.

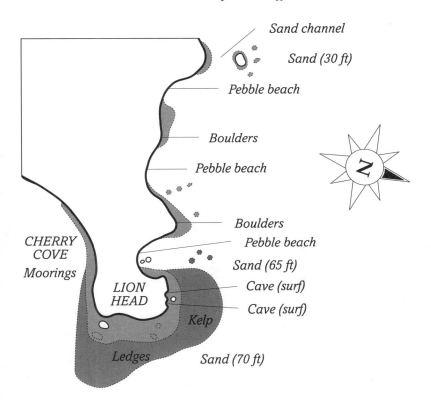

Sand channel

Sand (30 ft)

Pebble beach

Boulders

Pebble beach

Boulders

Pebble beach

Sand (65 ft)

Cave (surf)

Cave (surf)

CHERRY
COVE
Moorings

LION
HEAD

Kelp

Ledges

Sand (70 ft)

N

Lion Head looking southeast.

51

EAGLE REEF

*Area in three large sections covering
about 50 square yards.
White seabass, yellowtail and calico.
Beware of boat traffic and strong currents*

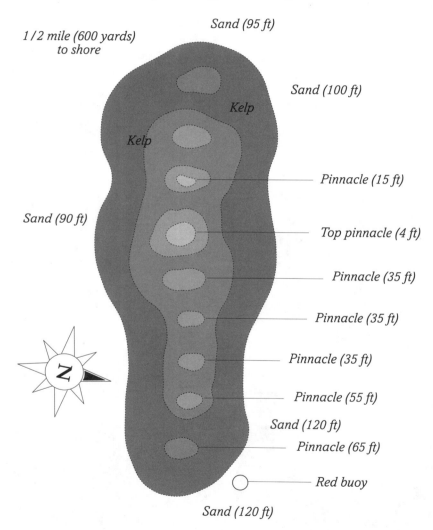

Sand (95 ft)

*1/2 mile (600 yards)
to shore*

Sand (100 ft)

Kelp

Kelp

Pinnacle (15 ft)

Sand (90 ft)

Top pinnacle (4 ft)

Pinnacle (35 ft)

Pinnacle (35 ft)

Pinnacle (35 ft)

Pinnacle (55 ft)

Sand (120 ft)

Pinnacle (65 ft)

Red buoy

Sand (120 ft)

1.5 miles SE to Lionhead   *1.5 miles NE to Ship Rock*

EEL COVE

Special closed area. Take no invertebrates.
Halibut and bat rays.

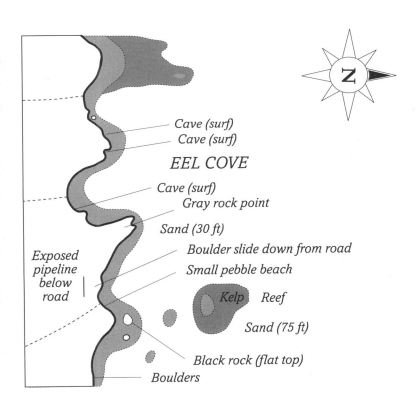

Cave (surf)
Cave (surf)

EEL COVE

Cave (surf)
Gray rock point

Sand (30 ft)

Exposed
pipeline
below
road

Boulder slide down from road

Small pebble beach

Kelp   Reef

Sand (75 ft)

Black rock (flat top)

Boulders

Flat black rock and Eel Cove looking southwest.

53

LITTLE & BIG GEIGER COVES

Special closed area. Take no invertebrates.
Good anchorage. Halibut.

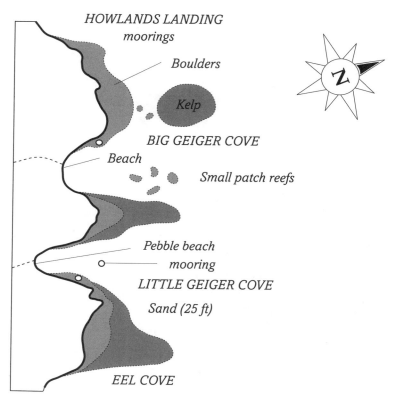

HOWLANDS LANDING
moorings

Boulders

Kelp

BIG GEIGER COVE

Beach

Small patch reefs

Pebble beach
mooring

LITTLE GEIGER COVE

Sand (25 ft)

EEL COVE

Little and Big Geiger Coves looking southwest.

HOWLANDS / EMERALD POINT

Special closed area. Take no invertebrates.
Good anchorage.
Halibut, yellowtail, calico and sheephead.

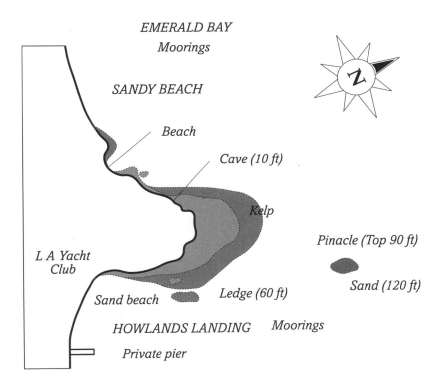

EMERALD BAY
Moorings

SANDY BEACH

Beach

Cave (10 ft)

Kelp

Pinacle (Top 90 ft)

L A Yacht
Club

Sand (120 ft)

Ledge (60 ft)

Sand beach

HOWLANDS LANDING   *Moorings*

Private pier

Howlands / Emerald point looking south.

INDIAN ROCK

Special closed area. Take no invertebrates. Good anchorage. Halibut, calico and sheephead.

EMERALD BAY
Johnson Landing

Moorings

Truck frame (60 ft)
(not much remains)

Kelp

Sand channel

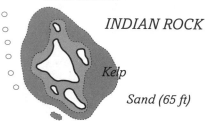

INDIAN ROCK

Kelp

Sand (65 ft)

Sand (35 ft)

Reef (40 ft)

Indian Rock looking north.

ARROW POINT

Surge and currents. Halibut, yellowtail, calico, sheephead and scallops.

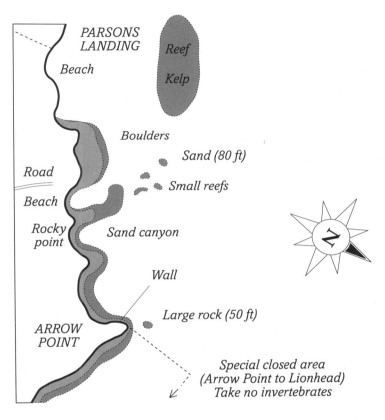

PARSONS
LANDING

Beach

Reef

Kelp

Boulders

Sand (80 ft)

Road

Small reefs

Beach

Rocky
point

Sand canyon

N

Wall

Large rock (50 ft)

ARROW
POINT

Special closed area
(Arrow Point to Lionhead)
Take no invertebrates

Arrow Point and Parsons Landing looking southeast.

BLACK POINT / JOHNSON'S ROCK

*Rocky. Lobster, scallops,
yellowtail, calico, sheephead and
angel sharks.*

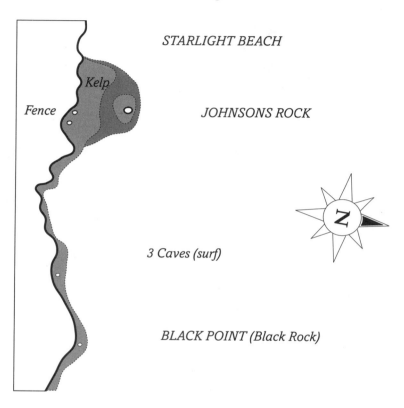

STARLIGHT BEACH

Kelp

Fence

JOHNSONS ROCK

3 Caves (surf)

BLACK POINT (Black Rock)

Starlight Beach and Johnsons Rock looking southwest.

WEST END (LANDS END)

Most exposed point of the island.
Heavy surf, surge and currents.
Gorgonians, lobster and scallops.

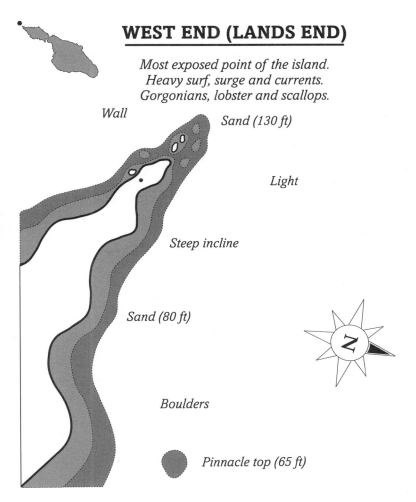

Wall

Sand (130 ft)

Light

Steep incline

Sand (80 ft)

Boulders

Pinnacle top (65 ft)

Land's End looking east.

EAGLE ROCK (FINGER ROCK)

*Gorgonians, calico, sheephead
and scallops. Large swell, surge
and currents.*

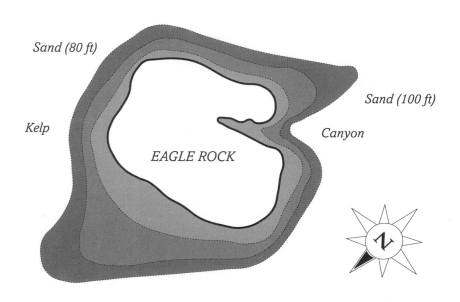

Sand (80 ft)

Sand (100 ft)

Kelp

Canyon

EAGLE ROCK

Eagle Rock. Looking northeast.

CACTUS BAY

Cactus Bay offers good anchorage in Santa Ana winds. Gorgonians, sheephead and some scallops.

CACTUS BAY (west side)

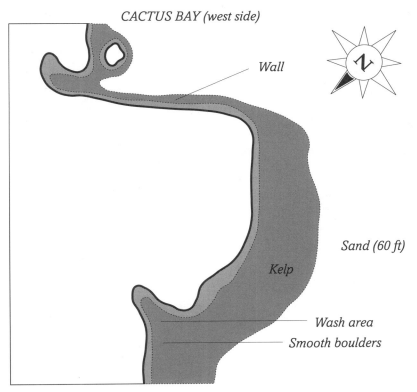

Wall

Sand (60 ft)

Kelp

Wash area

Smooth boulders

Western point of Cactus Bay looking northeast.

GULL ROCK / IRONBOUND COVE

Surge and currents. Good anchoring.
Halibut, sheephead and calico.
Squid spawn here in the spring.

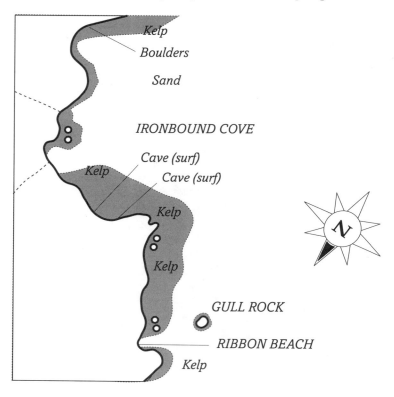

Kelp

Boulders

Sand

IRONBOUND COVE

Cave (surf)

Kelp

Cave (surf)

Kelp

Kelp

GULL ROCK

RIBBON BEACH

Kelp

Gull Rock looking east.

RIBBON ROCK

Named for quartz ribbons throughout dark rock. Walls, caves and ledges. Surge and currents. Deep anchoring. Yellowtail, sheephead, calico, scallops and some lobster.

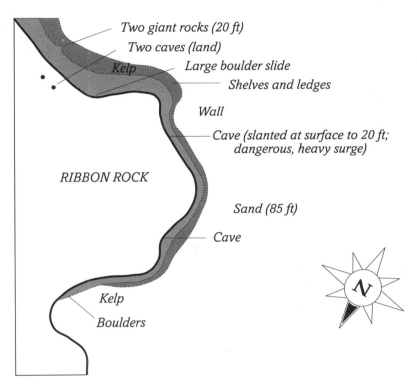

Two giant rocks (20 ft)

Two caves (land)

Kelp

Large boulder slide

Shelves and ledges

Wall

Cave (slanted at surface to 20 ft; dangerous, heavy surge)

RIBBON ROCK

Sand (85 ft)

Cave

Kelp

Boulders

N

Ribbon Rock looking northeast.

WHALE ROCK

Walls, currents and surge.
White seabass, yellowtail, calicos,
sheephead, lobster and scallops.

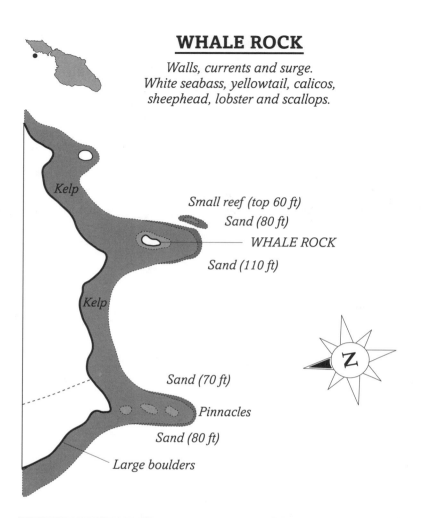

Small reef (top 60 ft)
Sand (80 ft)
WHALE ROCK
Sand (110 ft)

Kelp

Kelp

Sand (70 ft)

Pinnacles

Sand (80 ft)

Large boulders

Whale Rock looking northwest.

KELP POINT

Rocky point with surge and currents.
Some lobster and scallops.

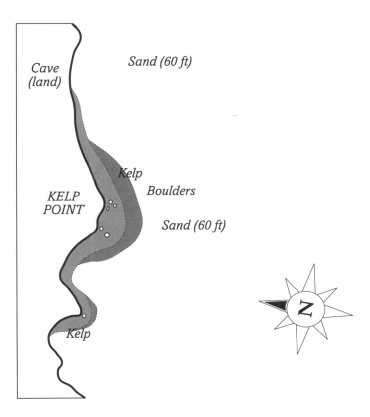

Cave
(land)

Sand (60 ft)

Kelp

KELP
POINT

Boulders

Sand (60 ft)

N

Kelp

Kelp Point looking northwest.

CAPE CORTEZ

Pinnacles, canyons and walls.
Surge and currents. Lobster,
scallops, calico and sheephead.

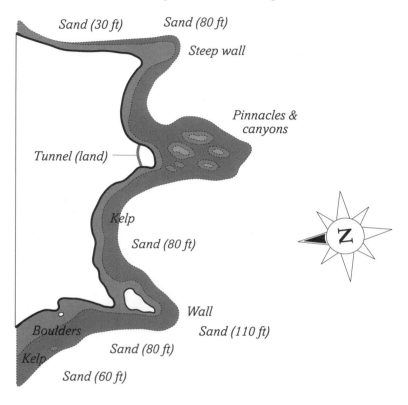

Sand (30 ft) Sand (80 ft)

Steep wall

Pinnacles &
canyons

Tunnel (land)

Kelp

Sand (80 ft)

Wall

Sand (110 ft)

Boulders

Sand (80 ft)

Kelp

Sand (60 ft)

N

Cape Cortes looking northwest.

LOBSTER BAY

Lobster, scallops, calico and sheephead.
Surge and currents.

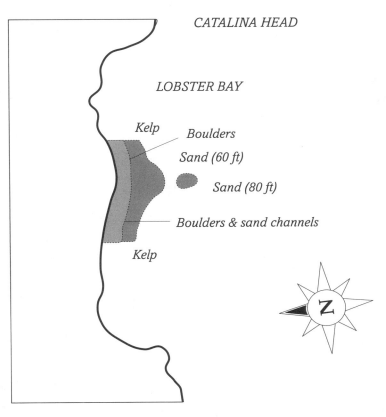

CATALINA HEAD

LOBSTER BAY

Kelp

Boulders

Sand (60 ft)

Sand (80 ft)

Boulders & sand channels

Kelp

Lobster Bay looking north.

67

CATALINA HEAD

*Caves and walls. Boat traffic, surge
and currents. Yellowtail, sheephead,
calico, lobster and some scallops.
Halfmoon and zebraperch.*

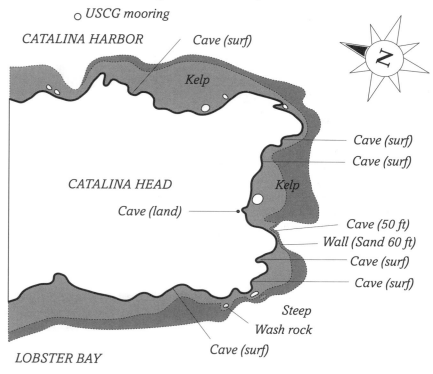

○ *USCG mooring*

CATALINA HARBOR

Cave (surf)

Kelp

Cave (surf)

Cave (surf)

CATALINA HEAD

Kelp

Cave (land)

Cave (50 ft)

Wall (Sand 60 ft)

Cave (surf)

Cave (surf)

Steep

Wash rock

Cave (surf)

LOBSTER BAY

Catalina Head looking north.

68

CATALINA HARBOR / PIN ROCK

Cat Harbor: Calm protected anchorage.
Several wrecks. Poor visibility in back harbor.
Beware of heavy boat traffic.
Pin Rock: Pinnacle with several giant rocks to East.
Steep walls surrounded by sand (35 - 45 ft).

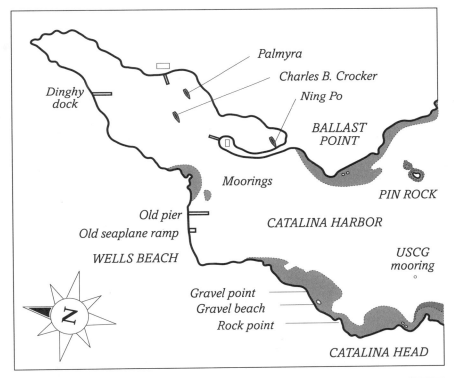

Pin Rock. Looking northwest.

PEDESTAL ROCK

Pinnacle about 200 yards off large boulder slide. Gorgonians. White seabass, yellowtail, calico, lobster and scallops.

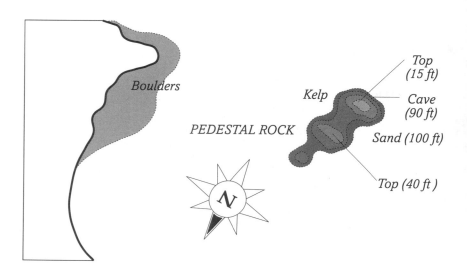

Boulders

Kelp

PEDESTAL ROCK

Top (15 ft)

Cave (90 ft)

Sand (100 ft)

Top (40 ft)

N

Pedestal Rock (at buoy) looking east toward point.

FRED ROCK

Discovered while diving with Fred.
33-23-65 N, 118-28-99 W.
Pinnacle about 150 yards off small beach.
Series of patchy reefs off point.
White seabass, yellowtail, calico, lobster and scallops.

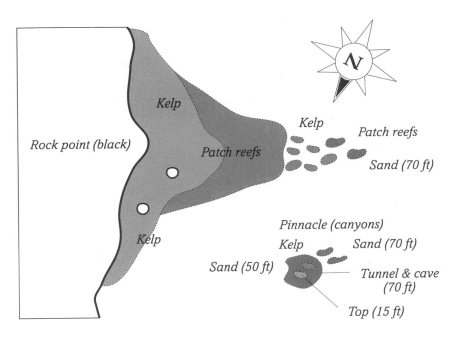

Rock point (black) looking east.

LITTLE HARBOR

Reef offers some protection for anchoring.
Beach diving and snorkeling.
Outside reef has some calico, sheephead,
lobster and scallops. Halibut in sand.

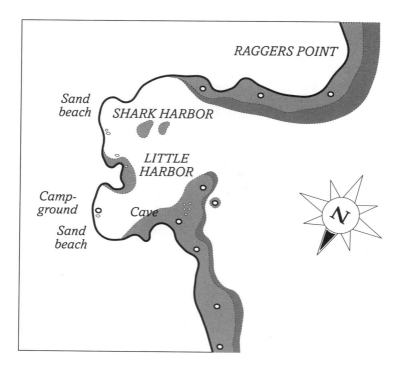

RAGGERS POINT

Sand
beach

SHARK HARBOR

LITTLE
HARBOR

Camp-
ground

Cave

Sand
beach

N

Little Harbor looking from top of Raggers Point.

72

SENTINEL ROCKS

*Exposed rocky points. Surge and poor
visibility. Yellowtail, calico, sheephead,
lobster and scallops.*

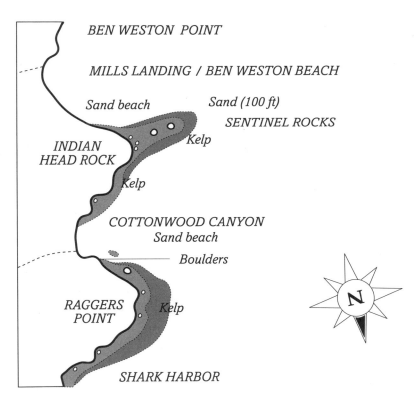

BEN WESTON POINT

MILLS LANDING / BEN WESTON BEACH

Sand beach

Sand (100 ft)

SENTINEL ROCKS

Kelp

INDIAN
HEAD ROCK

Kelp

COTTONWOOD CANYON
Sand beach

Boulders

RAGGERS
POINT

Kelp

SHARK HARBOR

N

Sentinel Rocks looking east.

FARNSWORTH BANK

Sheer walls, caves, canyons and valleys.

MARINE PRESERVE (No coral may be taken)

Covered by purple hydrocoral (best over 100 ft).
Avoid damage to reef when anchoring.
White seabass, yellowtail, blue rockfish and calico.
Beware of surf, surge, currents, depth and torpedo rays.

1.5 miles to Ben Weston
Point (235 mag)

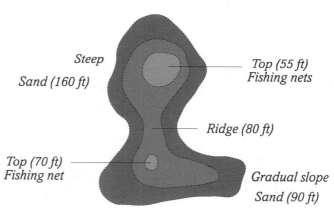

Steep

Sand (160 ft)

Top (55 ft)
Fishing nets

Ridge (80 ft)

Top (70 ft)
Fishing net

Gradual slope
Sand (90 ft)

To Catalina Harbor (319
mag)

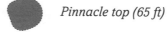

Pinnacle top (65 ft)

Pinnacle top (80 ft)

CHINA POINT

Named for camp used to smuggle illegal Chinese. Numerous rocky points. Reefs off beaches along coast. Heavy surf, surge and currents. Poor visibility. Island may block VHF radio. White seabass, yellowtail, calico, sheephead, lobster and some scallops. Sea lions and seals.

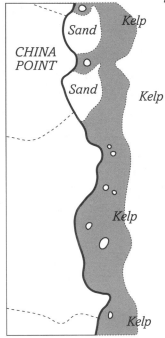

China Point looking east.

SALTA VERDE POINT

Scattered rock piles. Surge and poor visibility.
Island may block VHF radio.
Halibut, white seabass, yellowtail and calico.
Black seabass (protected)

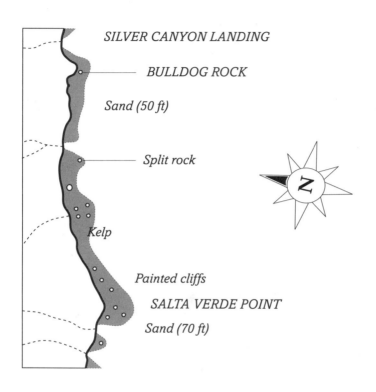

SILVER CANYON LANDING

BULLDOG ROCK

Sand (50 ft)

Split rock

Kelp

Painted cliffs

SALTA VERDE POINT

Sand (70 ft)

Salta Verde Point looking west.

CHURCH ROCK

Also called Cathedral Rock.
Caves and rock piles. Poor visibility.
Island may block VHF radio.
Lobster, scallops, white seabass, yellowtail and calico.

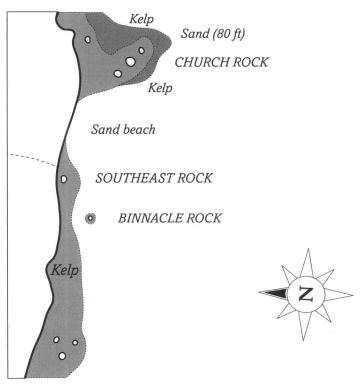

Church Rock looking northeast.

III. GAME

Basic information on how to catch, clean and cook
lobster, abalone, scallops and fish.

LOBSTER

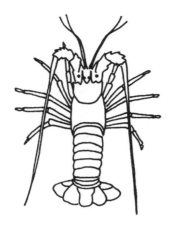

CALIFORNIA SPINY LOBSTER

Red with spines pointing
foreward. Length to 36".

Night diving at Catalina exposes many of the creatures that hide during the day. The tastiest is the *California Spiny Lobster* or "bug." By day, lobster usually sit near the entrance of a hole with antenae sticking out. However at night, they tend to venture out searching the bottom for scraps of food. Bugs have poor eyesight but do sense changes in light, water vibrations and chemical scents. When mating the male deposits a gray paste on the stomach of the female. The female may lay thousands of eggs but few will survive the ten years required to reach legal size. Besides hiding, the bugs' main defense is its hard spiny shell and the use of rapid tail thrusts to swim away. About once each year the lobster will climb out of its shell and discard it (molt). The soft, defenseless body will later become hard during this growing phase. Molted shells are easy to catch but provide for poor dining.

Some special equipment will help. Divers can only take lobster by hand, so heavy flexible gloves are needed for protection. For searching at night have a powerful, wide angle, underwater light and a back up (just in case). Be sure to check the batteries before diving. To store the many anticipated bugs, take a game bag with attached lobster gauge to measure size. Roll up the bag and streamline any loose gear prior to diving. To assist in good search patterns a compass is also helpful.

Plan to dive at night or early morning. A night with little or no moon is best (experienced bug grabbers can also bag them by day). The less dived areas tend to produce the most bugs. If possible, a prior dive during the day will help determine bug populations. Plan to be the first divers in the water and avoid other divers for greater success.

When diving, search the rocky reefs near kelp beds and eel grass. Glide smoothly over and around the rocks while sweeping the light from side to side. Bugs often hide at night so look for antenae in holes, crevasses and under ledges. Use good search patterns and cover as much area as possible. If nothing is found at shallow depths, go deeper. When bugs are sighted at a certain depth, concentrate efforts in that range. If no lobster are sighted in a certain area, move somewhere else.

When a lobster is spotted, estimate the size before attempting to grab it. Surprise is the key, don't hesitate, grab it quickly! The light may stun the bug for a few seconds. Aim for the joint where the back and tail meet. Try to pin the bug to the bottom. When the bug is in a hole, first check for urchins, eels and scorpionfish. Thrust hand into the top of the hole and grab the back or base of antenae. If the bug gets stuck in the hole, shaking may disorient and dislodge it. Bugs that are too deep in a hole should be passed over.

Once in hand, measure across the back with the lobster gauge. Beware of the large spines that line the edge of the tail. Release bugs that are too short. Try to avoid breaking the legs and antenae of shorts which causes disability. If legal size, roll up the tail and place in the bag tail first. Be careful not to let any other bugs escape. Teamwork can be effective by designating a bagger and catcher, then switching positions. Often, a bug in a hole may have a back door for escape. This is a good place to position a second diver.

Remember to be courteous and quiet to other boaters at night. Stay out of commercial lobster traps. Lobster fisherman are not allowed to trap the frontside of the island and are just trying to make a living. Practice conservation by taking only what is needed and replace any females with eggs. Good luck!

LOBSTER CLEANING

Remove the tail from the lobster body by rolling tail in, then grab tail and body at carapace and twist in opposite directions and pull apart.

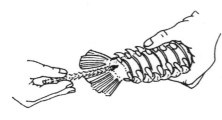

To remove intestinal vein break off about half the antenae. Stick the broken end of antenae in the anal hole. Push in, twist and pull antenae out to remove the vein. Roll lobster tail and freeze if desired.

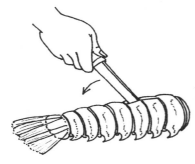

To split lobster tail lengthwise, lay tail with back facing up. Carefully pierce back of shell with stiff knife and force down to split in half. Remove vein if not done prior.

LOBSTER COOKING

GRILLED LOBSTER

Lobster: Tails cleaned and split in half lengthwise.
Herbs: Garlic, parsley, paprika,etc.
Butter and Lemon

Directions: Place tail halves, shell side down, on hot grill and cook about 8 minutes. Baste meat with butter to keep moist. Turn and cook about 6 minutes (don't overcook, meat will turn white when done). Melt butter and add garlic and parsley (if desired). Glaze meat with melted butter and light sprinkle of paprika (perhaps a dash of tabasco). Serve hot with melted herb butter and lemon wedges.

BOILED LOBSTER

Lobster: Whole live or tail.

Directions: Drop whole live lobster or tail into boiling water. Size of lobster determines cooking time (1 lb./about 8 minutes; 2 lbs./about 12 minutes ; 3 to 5 lbs./about 15 minutes). Cook until bright red (don't overcook).
Serve with melted butter and lemon wedges (see above)..

LOBSTER COCKTAIL

Lobster
Cocktail sauce: Store bought, old family recipe or page 101.
Celery
Lemon

Directions: Cook lobster (see boiled lobster). Let cool and refrigerate. Remove meat from shell and cut into small shredded chunks. Chop celery into fine pieces. Combine lobster, celery and cocktail sauce. Serve in small dishes and garnish with lemon wedges.

ABALONE

GREEN ABALONE

Oval flat-shaped shell
with 5 to 7 slightly raised holes.
Reddish-brown to dark green
color. Long olive green tentacles.
Some marine growth.

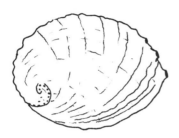

PINK ABALONE

Deeper, rounder shell with
2 to 6 volcano-like holes. Dull
red color with corrugated edge.
Lacy black and white
(peppered) tentacles. More
marine growth.

Abalone (ab) is a giant sea snail with a single ear-shaped shell. The shell is connected to a powerful muscle (foot), which secures it to a rock. Rimming the base of the shell are eyes and tentacles (mantle). Abalone don't see much more than shadows and changes in light but do sense water vibrations. As juveniles they move about, but as adults they tend to stay put. This home is a bare spot on a rock called a scar. Abalone move out at night to graze on algae, especially kelp, then return to the scar.

Abalone harvesting on Catalina goes back to the Indians over 5,000 years ago. Then abalone were plentiful, but now the population has dwindled. Today, few of the deep white abalone are ever seen and the "Withered Foot" disease has nearly wiped out the shallow black ab. Catalina still has green and pink abalone, but they are also in decline.

Best diving for abalone is from 10 to 70 feet deep (green: 10 to 30 feet; pink: 20 to 70 feet). When hunting abalone, search near the base of reefs with kelp and algae. Check out all cracks, crevasses, ledges and holes. Look for areas where broken kelp is deposited. Don't forget to look up; they may be on their side or upside down. The shell may be covered with marine growth, so look for unusual bumps or the mantle. A good ab diver has his fins sticking up and his head in a hole. Larger abalone may be loners, away from competition. Some big ones reside deep in holes with smaller abs protecting the entrance. When one ab is found, look around. There is a good change you may find another. Approach quietly. If the ab senses disturbed water or a shadow, it may clamp down making removal more difficult.

Abalone may only be taken with an approved ab iron and measuring device (see Fish & Game rules). Before removing, inspect the area for eels and urchins. Measure the abalone if possible. Knowing hand size will give a rough estimate. To remove, observe how the ab sits on the rock, then slip the ab iron between the foot and rock and flip up. Pushing down on the iron may injure the ab. Abalone are hemophiliacs and even a small cut may cause it to bleed to death. After removal, remeasure the ab. If it's too short, replace it at the same spot and hold in place to allow resuction.

Local commercial abalone divers began restocking Catalina with juvenile abs. This effort has been continued by the Catalina Conservancy Divers (see Catalina Diving Directory, page 102). Because of the decline of abalone in Catalina, information on dive site locations will not be provided. You'll have to find them on your own!

ABALONE CLEANING

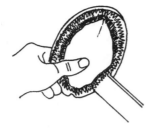

Slide an abalone iron between the meat and shell to shuck.

Make a V-shaped cut at the head and remove the guts. Search the stomach for abalone pearls (small rounded pieces of shell).

Trim the tentacles from the muscle. Tentacles may be scrubbed, cut in pieces and used in chowder or burgers.

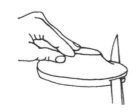

Carefully slice the meat into 1/8 - 1/4 inch steaks and discard the bottom foot.

Pound the steaks on both sides with an abalone hammer. Pound in a circular pattern, in to out to tenderize. Avoid pounding holes through the meat.

ABALONE COOKING

ABALONE STEAKS

Abalone: Pounded into steaks.
Milk   Seasoned bread crumbs, crackers or corn flakes.
Egg: Beaten. Oil and butter: Equal amounts.

Directions: Dry ab steaks on paper towel. Mix milk and egg. Dip ab into mix then coat with breading and fry in hot oil or butter until brown (about 30 to 60 seconds on each side). Dry on paper towels and serve hot as main dish or in sandwiches.

ABALONE KABOBS

Abalone: Pounded into steaks.
Mushrooms, bell peppers, onions, cherry tomatoes, etc...
Olive oil
Wood skewers: Soaked in water to avoid burning.

Directions: Fold ab steaks over several times and place on skewers with choice of vegetables. Place on hot grill and baste with olive oil to keep moist. Serve hot.

ABALONE BURGERS

Abalone: Ground up (save the juice).
Seasoned bread crumbs or "Nature Burger" mix.
Milk and egg
Onion and bell pepper: 1/4 cup minced.
Oil and butter: Equal amounts.

Directions: Combine ingredients together and form into patties and chill in refrigerator. Fry in hot oil and butter until golden brown. Serve on toasted bun with lettuce and mayonaise or whatever. This avoids pounding and makes a little abalone go a long way.

SCALLOPS

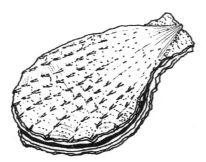

ROCK SCALLOP

Spiny brown/orange top shell, often covered with heavy marine growth. Bottom shell cemented to rock. Inside shell is white with purple hinge. Mantle is orange or olive green. Length to 6".

For a good game of hide and seek, try diving for scallops. Half the shell is cemented to rock so they're easy to catch. The hard part is trying to find them. Scallops tend to shy away from direct sunlight by attaching to cracks, crevasses, cliff faces and overhangs. Encrusted by heavy marine growth, they blend into the surroundings and are masters of camoflage. Filter feeding requires the scallop to open its shell (lips) slightly. Separation of the lips exposes the mantle or "scallop smile." The smile is pink/orange or dull green in color. This contrast against the marine background provides the best way to spot them.

Searching for scallops requires good buoyancy control and a smooth silent approach. Scan the area foreward while kicking easily. Stay off the rocks. Scallops will close if a shadow crosses or the water vibrations surrounding them is disturbed. When a scallop is seen, note the location, if they close, they can hide right in front of your face. Before removing look for other scallops as they tend to come in groups.

To remove, slip a knife, ab iron or large screwdriver between where the shell is cemented to the rock and pry off. Ability to remove scallops can vary from easy to almost impossible. Avoid spending too much time on difficult scallops. There is no size limit, but scallops smaller than palm size are not worth the effort. Collecting scallops is like putting rocks into the game bag, so be aware of buoyancy changes. Some divers use a thin bladed knife to slip in between the shells and remove only the innards. This technique avoids the heavy game bag but if the scallop is cut in half, Fish and Game will count them as two scallops. There is no closed season for scallops which provides a year-round game of hide and seek. The diver who wins this game is rewarded with a very tasty meal.

TYPICAL SCALLOP LOCATIONS

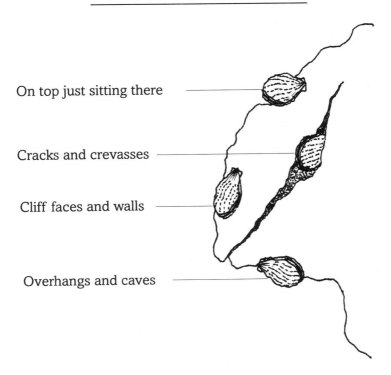

On top just sitting there

Cracks and crevasses

Cliff faces and walls

Overhangs and caves

SCALLOP CLEANING

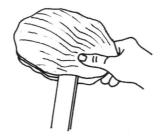

Slip a thin knife between the shells, then scrape the aductor muscle (button) from the flat shell and pull the shell halves apart.

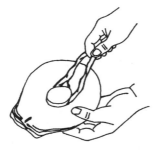

With the button still attached to the shell half, use fingers to remove the guts.

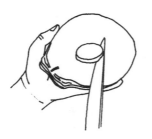

Scrape the button away from the shell.

Trim the small, hard, white portion from the button. Scrub off any remaining brown (guts) and rinse.

SCALLOP COOKING

SCALLOP SCAMPI

Scallops: Rinsed, patted dry and cut into 1/4 pieces.
Garlic: One clove minced
Onion: 3 tablespoons minced
Taragon: 2 teaspoons minced
Lemon juice: 1 teaspoon
Unsalted butter: 3 tablespoons

Directions: Heat 1-1/2 T. butter over medium high heat. Sauté scallops about 1 minute then remove. Add other ingredients and cook until onion is soft. Replace scallops and cook until heated through. Good over pasta.

SCALLOP KABOBS

Scallops: Large ones cut in half.
Skewers: Metal or wood (soak in water 1-2 hours).
Bell peppers, onions, mushrooms, cherry tomatoes etc...
Basting sauce: Soy with a little ginger, garlic & lemon.

Directions: Place scallops and vegetables on skewers. Place on hot oiled grill for about 4 minutes. Turn and baste with sauce.

SCALLOPERONI PIZZA

Scallops: thinly sliced.
Pizza crust: or french bread or "Boboli", etc...
Vegies: Onions, bell peppers, mushrooms, olives, etc...
Cheese: Mozzarella and parmesan.
Sauce: Pesto or tomato

Directions: Cover crust with sauce. Add vegetable toppings and cheese. Bake in oven until crust is brown. Remove and add scallop slices (ground abalone or lobster chunks are also tasty). Sprinkle on parmesan cheese. Replace in oven and cook about 6 to 8 minutes. This makes a little seafood go a long way.

SPEARFISHING: OPEN OCEAN

WHITE SEABASS

Large silver croaker,
Lower jaw extends past
upper jaw.
Length to 70".

YELLOWTAIL

Horizontal stripe from
eye to tail. Tail is
yellow/green color.
Length to 60".

White seabass and yellowtail are the premier gamefish of Catalina free divers. These open ocean fish are easily alerted by SCUBA bubbles, so breath-hold diving is the best method of hunting.

Most free diving equipment will double for use in SCUBA diving. A low volume good fitting mask uses less air to clear. Size and type of fins are determined by an individual's strength and ability. Snorkels should be large bore for easy breathing. Weight belts must be well balanced, snug fitting and comfortable with the quick release set opposite of the gun hand. Wear at least one glove for fish handling. Carry a good sharp knife to cut any tangled line. The speargun should be long and powerful for penetration and accuracy. Most pros prefer rubber band powered guns with wood stocks (metal tends to amplify noise). Trailing surface floats attached to the gun for retrieval and reels for extra line are helpful. Use double barbed detachable tips with long wings and keep them sharp. For safety, never cock the gun out of the water. Have a buddy hand the gun in and out of the boat and cover the tip with cork or rubber when not in use.

Free diving skills must be practiced and developed before hunting becomes efficient. Get in shape; good physical condition is important. First make a few short dives to purge the wetsuit of excess air.

Take a maximum of 2 to 3 deep breaths (don't hyperventilate!). Plan the breath for the entire dive, leaving enough air in reserve for the trip back to the surface. Be comfortable and keep mind and body relaxed. Avoid gasping for air at the surface. Rest a few minutes between dives. Find a good working depth and set the weight belt to neutral at that depth. The objective is not to dive deep but to get fish. Leg cramps may occur from fatigue or fins that are too large. If this happens rest on the surface and use fingers to massage the cramp or try holding the tip of the fin and straighten the leg. If cramps persist, call it quits for the day. Speargun accuracy should be practiced before diving. Try shooting at kelp leaves or a suspended plastic bottle.

Hunting is best in the spring when fish move into shallow water to spawn. Search the outside edges and channels of kelp beds, pinnacles and the seaward side of rocky points. These open water predators are difficult to spot, approach and shoot. The slightest movement or noise will alert the fish, causing it to instantly disappear. A colony defense system enables a single fish to quickly warn all others. Observing fish reactions in different situations and learning from mistakes provides the best way to develop hunting techniques.

When stalking, move slowly and silently using a smooth flutter kick. Drift or glide when possible. While surface scouting, breathe quietly and slowly move head from side to side. To submerge, use a smooth pike dive without using the arms. Remove the snorkel during descent to avoid bubbles, replace on ascent and clear using headroll technique. While underwater, use any available cover (kelp, reef, etc.). Focus on fish or other specific objects to maintain reference. Keep the gun ready and steady at eye level with arm fully extended. There is very little time to prepare a shot and any movement will alert the fish. Aim at a spot just behind the gill plate at the center of the spine. Squeeze the trigger as soon as the fish is lined up. Take only a good clear shot. A wounded fish can't be followed and will be lost. Once shot, go after the fish and prepare for a fight. Grab in the gills or put thumb and finger in eye sockets and hold tight to body to avoid thrashing. Boat the fish, then gut and place on ice ASAP.

SPEARFISHING: COASTAL

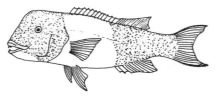

SHEEPHEAD (Male)

Fish begin as females (dull pink with white belly) then evolve into males. Head is black with blunt forehead, large protruding buck teeth and white chin. Middle of body is red. Tail is black. Length to 36".

KELP BASS (Calico)

Brown/green camoflaged color with yellowish blotches on back. Length to 26".

Coastal spearfishing concentrates on those fish that live in and around kelp, reefs, rock outcroppings, pilings and wrecks. Several types of fish inhabit the reefs and kelp. Calico bass are very tasty. They may rest in crevasses or be found swimming in the kelp. They are a cunning, "streetwise" fish that spooks easily. Forget trying to chase them! There is a size and bag limit so check Fish and Game regulations. Sheephead can get very large but the best eating size is about 14 to 18 inches. Several types of bottom dwelling rockfish can be found including olive (Johnny bass; similar to calico), vermillion (rock cod; deep water) and a few blue rockfish (Farnsworth Bank). Sculpin are very tasty but have venomous spines (see Hazardous Marine Life) which makes handling difficult and may be best avoided. In addition to sculpin, an occasional cabezon or lingcod may be found camoflaged in crevasses or on the bottom. White seabass and yellowtail may visit the fringes and channels of the kelp bed. These fish along with sargo, croaker, ocean whitefish and several types of perch provide a variety of hunting.

Equipment suited to kelp and rock is helpful. A pole spear with multi-tined or paralyser tip can be used for small fish. Most hunters prefer to go after larger fish with a short to medium-sized speargun. Thick rock pointed tips are recommended. Double wings for larger fish and a spinner head to prevent the fish from twisting off is effective. The line can be modified with a 1/8 inch stainless cable on the first section to avoid chaffing the shock line on rocks (replace if kinked). SCUBA divers may wish to adapt the gun to negative buoyancy so it can be set down on the bottom. Carrying a small light can be useful in caves and crevasses.

Many of the open ocean, free diving, hunting techniques may be used or adapted for SCUBA. Hunting underwater can be similar to hunting on land. Stalk or float quietly in the open channels of the kelp bed waiting for fish to swim by. Use rocks and kelp for cover during descent or while hunting. Move slowly and quietly with gun extended and ready. Try getting under the fish and shooting up. Aim at a spot behind the gill plate and into the spine. Large sheephead have thick scales and are best shot from behind. Search the bottom, caves and crevasses for rockfish. Spotting fish takes time and patience. Look over an area carefully and the hidden objects (fish) will appear. Line up the shot to avoid direct impact with rocks. Allow enough distance for the spear shaft to exit the end of the speargun. Use caution when buddy diving in kelp. Know the location of other divers to avoid accidents.

Once speared, place small fish in a game bag or on a stringer before removing from the shaft. Stringers may be attached to the diver using a quick release or to a surface float. Larger fish should be beached or boated. Gut and place fish on ice ASAP. Keep a log of fish observations for future reference. Be a hunter and not a killer. Take only what is needed and help preserve the fish populations.

SPEARFISHING: SAND BOTTOM

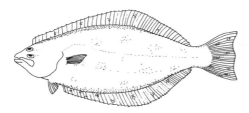

CALIFORNIA HALIBUT

Mottled gray/brown on top and white on bottom. Lateral line forms high arch over pectoral fin. Length to 60".

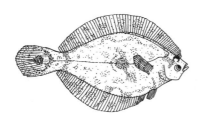

TURBOT

Lives on sand or rock bottom. Body is rounded, mottled grayish-brown on top and white on bottom. Round bug-eyes. Length to 14".

Though desert-like in appearance, the sandy bottom offers a hunting challenge. Sand bass, deep dwelling rock cod and turbot call the sand home, but the prize is halibut. A halibut is a flatfish which lays on the bottom waiting for food to swim by. Juvenile halibut begin life swimming about. During growth, they move to the bottom and their eyes shift to one side (usually left). The underside transforms to a pale white and the top side becomes grayish-brown which can change color to match its surroundings. Halibut lay camoflaged on the bottom and may partially bury themselves in a fine layer of sand. Although they live on the bottom, halibut are not bottom feeders. With its large mouth and sharp teeth, it rises off the bottom in an explosive lunge to grab squid, anchovies and other small fish.

During the winter, halibut are found in deep water (to 200 feet). From February to July they move toward shore (5 to 15 feet) to spawn and feed and may stay till early fall. They will often move in shallow during a grunion run. Hunting is best in the early evening or morning. Halibut can be found in the channels leading to bays and off long beaches (often bordered by rocks and eel grass). Large ones can be found between rock outcroppings, arround pilings, wrecks and moorings. Halibut can be hunted by free diving or SCUBA. A pole spear can be used but a small to medium high powered speargun is best. A rock point with double wings and a detachable head is very effective.

When hunting, move slowly and quietly over the bottom as far as visibility permits. Cover a lot of ground quickly. Drift or glide whenever possible and keep the speargun ready. Swimming into the sun gives greater visibility and avoids casting a shadow. Look for distinctive halibut shaped outlines or an unusual oval-shaped mound of sand. Search for two eyes staring up. Often, the fins (especially the tail) will remain exposed. A cloud of mud (sand explosion) is usually a sign of a spooked halibut or other bottom dweller. Halibut shaped depressions or prints may indicate a good area. When signs of halibut or sightings occur, concentrate on that area and depth.

When sighted, keep the gun aimed at the eyes. Slowly move in for the shot. Often a halibut will rely on its camoflage and let a diver pass over -- but don't wait too long to shoot. Aim for the spot just behind the gill plate and through the spine. Leave enough distance for the shaft to exit the end of the speargun. A halibut is a powerful fish (average weight is 5 to 20 pounds) so expect a fight. Use body weight to pin the fish to the bottom. With the fish still on the shaft, rip out the gills to disable the fish. The halibut can now be boated, beached or placed on a stringer. Gut and place on ice ASAP.

FISH CLEANING

FILLETING

Make the first cut just behind the gills and slice down diagonally toward the head. Cut to the bone, but not into the guts.

Turn the blade and slide it along the backbone toward the tail while pulling the meat away from the fish. Turn the fish over and repeat on the other side.

Slide the knife along the rib bones and remove the rib section from both fillets.

Cut a 1/2 inch wedge at the tail for a finger grip. Keep the knife at an angle and shave the meat from the skin. Lightly rinsed fillets are now ready for use.

DRESSING

Make the first cut just behind the gills and slice down diagonally toward the head. Cut to the bone. Cut belly from tail to head (don't cut too deep). Use finger along spine to remove guts. Scale fish using back of knife and rinse. Cut off head, tail and fins and rinse.

STEAKING

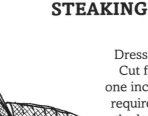

Dress fish as shown above. Cut fish in sections about one inch thick. Thick fish may require using a mallet to tap the knife through the bone. Rinse sections with water before use.

FLATFISH

Make the first cut just behind the gills and slice down diagonally toward the head to the bone. Cut along the dorsal fin. Separate the meat from the bones by sliding the knife along the bones to the spine. Slice the meat away from the spine and continue toward the belly. Flip fish over and repeat on other side.

FISH COOKING

BLACKENED FISH

Fish: About 2 pounds of fillets.

Herbs: 1 T. chili powder; 2 tsp. black pepper; 1 tsp. white pepper; 1 tsp. thyme; 1 tsp. onion powder; 1 tsp. paprika; 1/2 tsp. cayenne pepper; 1 tsp. garlic powder; 1 tsp. basil.

Lemon Wedges. Butter and oil: Equal amounts.

Directions: Mix herbs together and sprinkle on fish. Fry fish in hot oil skillet. Cook until crisp on outside (about 4 to 5 minutes per side). Can be placed on hot oiled BBQ grill (5 to 7 minutes per side) instead of skillet. Best cooked outside due to smoke. Serve hot with lemon wedges and tartar sauce.

PAN FRIED CALICO

Fish: fillet and pat dry with paper towel.
Cut larger fillets into smaller portions.
Bread or cracker crumbs: 1 cup (or cornmeal or flour).
Salt and pepper: 1/2 teaspoon of each.
Egg
Milk: 1 T.   Butter and oil: Equal amounts.

Directions: Mix salt, pepper, egg and milk together. Dip fillet in mixture and coat with cracker crumbs. Fry fish in hot oil and butter until brown (about 2 to 3 minutes per side). Place on paper towel to remove excess oil. Serve hot with tartar sauce.

FISH TACOS

Fish: cut into chunks.   Taco shells: or corn tortillas
Toppings: cilantro, cheese, lettuce, salsa, sour cream

Directions: cook fish chunks then dry on paper towel. Place fish in warmed taco shells and add desired toppings.

GRILLED HALIBUT

Halibut: Filleted or steaked
Mayonaise
Herbs: Garlic, tarragon, thyme, dill, basil, sage and parsley
(experiment with combinations)

Directions: Spread mayonaise on one side of halibut and sprinkle on herbs of choice. Place on hot oiled grill, mayonaise side down. Cook about 5 minutes on each side per inch thickness of fish . Turn fish and repeat on other side. Mayo will keep fish moist but not mask the flavor. Serve hot.

SHEEPHEAD COCKTAIL

Sheephead: filleted.

Directions: Heat butter until clear then add lemon juice and garlic and fish and cook about 2 minutes or until fish turns white. Remove and place on paper towel. Chill in refrigerator overnight. Separate into chunks and add cocktail sauce or use in dishes similar to crab.

TARTAR SAUCE

Mayonaise and sour cream: 1/2 cup each.
Onion, garlic, sweet pickle, green olives, capers and parsley.
Your choice,One diced T. of each.
Lemon juice: 1 tsp.

Directions: Mix all ingredients and chill about 1 hour.

COCKTAIL SAUCE

Ketchup or chili sauce: 1/2 cup.
Lemon juice: 2 T.
Horseradish: 2 tsp.
Onion: 1 T. diced.
Worchestershire sauce: 1 tsp.

Directions: Mix it all up (dash of Tabasco) and chill 1 hour.

IV. APPENDIX

Information on diving services, safe diving, emergency procedures, bibliography and index.

CATALINA DIVING DIRECTORY

ARGO DIVING SERVICE
P.O. Box 2289
Avalon, Ca. 90704
Tours and instruction
Charter *Argo*
(310) 510-2208

AVALON AQUATICS
615 Crescent Ave.
P.O. Box 2362
Avalon, Ca. 90704
Full service
(310) 510-1225

CATALINA DIVERS SUPPLY
Pleasure Pier
P.O. Box 126
Avalon, Ca. 90704
Full service
Charter *Cat Dive*
(310) 510-0330

CATALINA MAKO
P.O. Box 2350
Avalon, Ca. 90704
Charter *Catalina Mako*
(310) 510-2720

CATALINA SCUBA LUV
126 Catalina
Avalon, Ca. 90704
Full service
(310) 510-2350

ISLAND CHARTERS
P.O. Box 1017
Avalon, Ca. 90704
Charter *King Neptune*
(310) 510-2616

WEST END DIVE CENTER
P.O. Box 5044
Two Harbors, Ca. 90704
Full service
Charter *Garibaldi*
(310) 510-2800

SAFE DIVING PRACTICES

1. GET IN SHAPE.
Diving can be physically and mentally exhausting. Be prepared.

2. MAINTAIN GOOD DIVING SKILLS.
Continuing education and practice.

3. USE WELL MAINTAINED EQUIPMENT.
Including a submersible pressure gauge, buoyancy compensator
with inflator and alternate air source. Inspect gear prior to diving.

4. AVOID USING DRUGS AND ALCOHOL.

5. PLAN THE DIVE.
Review emergency procedures, buddy system, dive sites
and conditions. Observe all local laws including dive flags,
Fish and Game regulations.

6. NO DECOMPRESSION DIVES.
Most everything is 60 feet deep or less. Know how to use the
dive tables. Ascend at proper rate. Plan and use safety stops.

7. PRACTICE GOOD BUOYANCY CONTROL.
Adjust weight belt for easy release. Don't overweight.
Use relaxed breathing (never hold your breath).
Avoid skip breathing and hyperventilation.

8. DIVE WITHIN PERSONAL ABILITY.
Avoid overexertion.

9. USE SURFACE SUPPORT.
If possible use a float or boat.

10. USE GOOD JUDGMENT.
Common sense, knowledge and training will help to avoid panic.

EMERGENCY DIVING PROCEDURES

Several agencies provide guidelines in emergency situations.
Divers Alert Network (DAN) is considered the leader. The
procedures listed below are a simple one page outline adapted
for Catalina Island. Review emergency plans prior to diving.

---

1. FLOTATION
Inflate the buoyancy compensator and drop the weight belt.

2. CALL FOR HELP.
Signal or yell for help. If possible, have someone contact Baywatch.

3. GET TO THE BOAT OR SHORE.
Aiding a victim in the water is difficult.

4. MAINTAIN AIRWAY, BREATHING AND CIRCULATION (ABC):
Lay the victim on his back. An unconscious victim may require
CPR or First Aid. If nauseated, roll onto either side. Treat for shock.
If embolism is suspected, elevate the legs a few inches.

5. CONTACT EMERGENCY SERVICES.
Contact (VHF radio) Baywatch or U.S. Coast Guard or
Harbor Patrol. Remember to state that it is a "diving emergency."
Give the location and type of vessel.

6. ADMINISTER OXYGEN.
If available.

7. GET MEDICAL ATTENTION.
Follow directions of emergency agencies or transport to
nearest medical facility.

8. KEEP VITAL INFORMATION.
Note dive history, time and personal information.
Keep all equipment together.

EMERGENCY SERVICES

On Catalina, several emergency services are available to serve the needs of divers and boaters. Primary response is provided by Baywatch Avalon or Baywatch Isthmus (Los Angeles County Lifeguard/Paramedic rescue boats). Avalon Harbor Patrol and Isthmus Harbor Patrol boats will assist in emergencies. The United States Coast Guard maintains rescue boats and helicopters nearby. Diving emergencies are relayed to the Catalina Hyperbaric Chamber located at Fisherman's Cove, near the Isthmus.

EMERGENCY AT SEA:
VHF may not reach local agencies from backside of the island or inside coves

If close to Avalon: Baywatch Avalon (VHF Channel 12 or 16).
                       Avalon Harbor Patrol (VHF Channel 12 or 16).

If close to Isthmus: Baywatch Isthmus (VHF Channel 09 or 16).
                       Isthmus Harbor Patrol (VHF Channel 09).

Other areas: United States Coast Guard (VHF Channel 16).

EMERGENCY ON LAND: DIAL 911
Cellular phones may transfer to the mainland. State your exact location.

EMERGENCY TELEPHONE NUMBERS:

Baywatch Avalon . . . . (310) 510-0856
Baywatch Isthmus . . . . (310) 510-0341
U.S. Coast Guard . . . . (310) 980-4444
Sheriff Avalon . . . . (310) 510-0174
Sheriff Isthmus . . . . (310) 510-0872
Harbor Patrol Avalon . . . . (310) 510-0535
Harbor Patrol Isthmus . . . . (310) 510-2683
Catalina Hyperbaric Chamber . . . . (310) 510-1053
Divers Alert Network (DAN) . . . . . (919) 684-8111

Remember to state the type of emergency.

BIBLIOGRAPHY

Berman, Bruce D. 1972. *Encyclopedia Of American Shipwrecks.* Mariners Press, Boston.

Dawson, E. Yale. 1972. *Seashore Plants Of Southern California.* University of California Press, Berkeley and Los Angeles.

Eschmeyer, William M. and Earl S. Herald. 1983. *A Field Guide to Pacific Coast Fishes North America.* Houghton Mifflin Co., Boston.

Gibbs, James A. 1962. *Shipwrecks Of The Pacific Coast.* 2nd Ed. Binfords and Mort, Portland.

Gotshall, Daniel W. 1981. *Pacific Coast Inshore Fishes.* 2nd Rev. Ed. Sea Challengers, Monterey.

Gotshall, Daniel W. and Laurence L. Laurent. 1979. *Pacific Coast Subtidal Marine Inverebrates, A Fishwatcher's Guide.* Sea Challengers, Monterey.

Johnson, Myrtle E. and Harry J. Snook. 1967. *Seashore Animals Of The Pacific Coast.* Dover Publications Inc., New York.

Marshall, Don B. 1978. *California Shipwrecks.* Superior Publishing Co., Seattle.

Reish, Donald R. 1972. *Marine Life Of Southern California.* Reish, Los Alamitos.

INDEX

INDEX

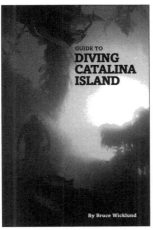

GUIDE TO

DIVING CATALINA ISLAND

By Bruce Wicklund

Please send _____ book(s) *Guide To Diving Catalina Island*. I understand that I may return the book for a full refund, for any reason, no questions asked.

Ship to:

NAME: _____

ADDRESS: _____

CITY: _____ STATE: _____ ZIP: _____

Book/s ($12.95 ea) _____

California Sales Tax (8.25%) _____

Shipping & Handling (First book $2.00) _____

Additional books $0.50 ea.) _____

TOTAL

Send check or money order (no cash) to:
Black Dolphin Diving
Box 5022, Avalon, CA 90704-5022.

Dealers, ask about wholesale rates.